Explaining
Fasting

Roger T. Forster

Bible quotations are taken from the NASB – New American Standard Bible
© The Lockman Foundation, 1960, 1962, 1963, 1968, 1971, 1972, 1973, 1975, 1977.
La Habra, California.

ISBN: 1 85240 126 5

SOVEREIGN WORLD LIMITED
P.O. Box 777, Tonbridge, Kent TN11 9XT, England.

Typeset and printed in the UK by Sussex Litho Ltd, Chichester, West Sussex.

Contents

Introduction

The subject of this book is hardly likely to be greeted with great enthusiasm by those of us living in our modern "consumer society". Indeed, those who are not so placed, but who are forced to exist in less economically favoured nations or communities, such will still question whether a title is appropriate or attractive for people in the world's current political, economic or even religious, popular philosophy.

However, before we turn to our Christian roots and revelation to ask questions concerning this subject, and before we take inspiration from our Christian mentors and spiritual giants of the past it is worth noting what many late twentieth-century believers have discovered when participating in this Christian discipline.

They have found in this ancient discipline *freedom* from our current crushing materialism, a *freshness* from the staid imprisonment of secular living, and a *fullness* of Christian experience in the midst of an empty lifestyle and existence. Of course it is Jesus, the Son of God himself, who is our freedom, freshness and fullness, but it is fasting which has often opened up for many the occasion of experiencing this fact with greater intensity and integrity than ever before.

John Wesley was one of the greatest Christian leaders and evangelists of eighteenth-century Britain. His work, under the Spirit of God, has been recognised by both Christian and secular historians to have changed the face of Britain. He rode a quarter of a million miles preaching Christ to the poor of his day and averted, on the territory of Britain, a revolution of bloodshed as was witnessed in eighteenth-century France. John Wesley, drawing on the wisdom of the early Church, said, "It was a common saying among the Christians of the primitive Church 'The soul and the body make the man; the Spirit and the disciplines make a Christian'." By this he implied that none could be real Christians without the help of disciplines. Further he added, "But if this is so, is there any wonder that we find so few Christians, for where is Christian discipline?"

When John Wesley bemoans the lack of Christians he is not

using the term simply as those who are born again (John 3:3, 5) or *'those who will reach heaven by faith in Christ's grace'*, but rather the name as in its biblical sense (it is a word found only three times in the New Testament: Acts 11:26, 26:28, 1 Peter 4:16); that is, it names someone who is a disciple or a learner of Christ. Those of us wishing to wear L plates for the rest of our lives are those qualifying as disciples of Jesus and may legitimately be named 'Christians' from a biblical point of view. These Christians, by the observation of John Wesley and the early Church, will practise disciplines.

It would appear that fasting is one of the three most important disciplines endorsed and advocated by Jesus in Matthew 6:1-18. Alongside prayer and giving, fasting is a means of laying hold of the grace that is in our Lord Jesus Christ. That these disciplines are not the ground upon which grace is given is clear from Jesus' teaching where he attacks the self-righteousness which such practices could produce.

Jesus shows the misuse of the disciplines is discerned in that their practitioners long to be seen by others; for instance "I am a great pray-er or giver or faster". These disciplines then are "our righteousness" not God's (*"Beware of practicing your righteousness before men"* Matthew 6:1) and are ever the danger points, therefore, of self-righteousness. Our attitude is to be like Paul's in Philippians 3:9 where he wishes to be found in Christ *"not having a righteousness of my own... but that which is through faith in Christ – the righteousness that comes from God."*

However, this gift of God did not prevent Paul from praying (*"The Lord said to* (Ananias), *'...enquire ...for a man from Tarsus named Saul, for behold he is praying'"* Acts 9:11), giving (*"I am going to Jerusalem, serving the saints. For Macedonia and Achaia have been pleased to make a contribution for the poor among the saints in Jerusalem,"* Romans 15:25, 26) and fasting (*"...there were in the* [Antioch] *church prophets and teachers* [Barnabas and Saul are named]. *While they were... fasting, the Holy Spirit said...,"* Acts 13:1, 2). If the ground of God's giving of his grace is Christ, the means of receiving and enjoying that grace is the disciplines.

Just as *"our righteousness"* (Matthew 6:1) is clearly not God's righteousness, *"...much more those who receive the gift of righteousness will reign in life through... Jesus Christ"* (Romans 5:17), so too our activity in sowing to the Spirit, to which Paul refers in Galatians 6:8 is not the wonderful activity of God's life which produces a harvest of the Spirit as in Galatians 5:22, but is merely our offering of the right conditions for such growth to take place from God.

These warnings or provisos concerning fasting may be summed up:

1) Because fasting is our righteousness not God's righteousness, it can lead to self-righteousness which is the great enemy of the Lord (Luke 12:1, John 19:7, Romans 10:3-5) destroying him and his life.

2) Fasting is but one of many disciplines,[1] not the only one disciples should practise as needful and central for experiential Christianity.

3) Fasting is a means of grace, not a ground of God's giving, but a means for receiving from the giver, the God of all grace.

If these warnings are noted then we may continue with safety into our inquiry concerning fasting.

[1]There are at least 19–20 disciplines, see article entitled Fasting in *The New Dictionary of Christian Ethics and Pastoral Theology*, forthcoming, IVP.

1

Jesus and
Fasting

"All Scripture is inspired by God and profitable for teaching, for reproof, correction, for training in righteousness; that the man of God may be adequate, equipped for every good work" (2 Timothy 3:16, 17).

When Paul asserts the profitability of all Scripture he is referring not only to the Old Testament called in verse 15 'Holy Scripture' which Timothy had known from his youth, but also the 'added things' Timothy had learnt from those he had known who were approved, as seen in verse 14. These were the apostles and others whose doctrine was accepted by them (Acts 2:42, John 14:26. The New Testament is the body of Apostolic Doctrine). Through these foundational teachers Timothy and we are able to understand the Old Testament in a Jesus way. We are converts to Jesus and we must learn from him how to understand all Scripture. The Old Testament Scriptures were to point to Jesus and not to be an end in themselves. Jesus (Matthew 5:17) comes to fulfil and so complete the Law. Without Jesus the Law can contradict (John 7:41-2, 8:5) and kill (John 19:7) as Paul reminds us in the phrase *"the letter that kills"* (2 Corinthians 3:6). But with Jesus and by the Spirit (John 16:13, 14) the Scripture, that is all Scripture, both Old and New, will be profitable and will give life (2 Corinthians 3:6). Understanding this is particularly important for the subject that we are examining, namely fasting.

Therefore, it is appropriate and necessary that we come to Jesus to see how he as a good Jew *"born under the Law"* (Galatians 4:4) interpreted the Old Testament for us with respect to fasting. It will be necessary to first look at the Old Testament background which lay behind the society in which Jesus lived and moved; to consider second what Jesus did and taught in the gospels and how he accepted the Old Testament practices; and third, to examine how the first Christians in the Acts of the Apostles and the Letters understood that the Spirit of Jesus was leading the Church to follow Jesus' example and teaching.

1. The Old Testament in the Light of Jesus

There are two[2] Old Testament words for fasting:

Sôm – to cover the mouth. This is clearly a reference to the refusal to eat or indeed drink (2 Samuel 1:12, Nehemiah 1:4).

Anah – to humble oneself. This word could be a synonym for *sôm*, but could also include such fasting as not eating, but drinking, refusing luxury foods or some particular foods for various purposes and reasons (Daniel 1:8-13, and compare Romans 14:21) as well as refusing fine clothes and pleasures (Psalm 35:13, 69:10, 11, Deuteronomy 8:3).

The Old Testament presented Jesus with at least four categories of fasting:

a) The Commanded Fast of the Law

It is surprising that there is only one commanded fast for the Old Testament people of God in the Law of Moses; that was the Day of Atonement.[3] The fasting for that one day would above all represent the seriousness and repentance necessary to receive the annual atonement or reconciliation with God when the scapegoat removed the sins of the people. The High Priest dismissed this goat to the desert having confessed the people's sins over the animal, while the blood of another goat was sprinkled in the Holy of Holies of Moses' tabernacle re-affirming the way back to a relationship with God. This day was also a sabbath day so the people of Israel had nothing to do – no works, in order to receive their atonement with God and from God (Leviticus 16:29-34, 23:26-32).

[2]*revath* is also used once in Daniel 6:18 and translated fasting.

[3]Leviticus 23:14 seems to be a partial fast also commanded through Moses.

10

Almost certainly Jesus would have fasted with the rest of the Jewish people on this day. We have no record of any accusations against him on this matter. It is however possible that his disciples were not so strict – *"John's disciples and the Pharisees were fasting; and some came and said to Jesus, 'Why do John's disciples and the disciples of the Pharisees fast, but your disciples do not fast?'"* (Mark 2:18), although this incident may refer to the extra voluntary fasts which will be examined also, and not necessarily the Atonement Day fast.

There seems to be little doubt that Jesus was to be understood as having fulfilled the one compulsory fast of the Law (Matthew 5:17). However, in the same way as it is well known that he challenged the old understanding of the sabbath, so also his crucifixion challenged and eliminated all blood sacrifices including those of the Day of Atonement. In his words the cross was *"a ransom price for many"* (Mark 10:45) which precluded any further sacrifices of blood: *"And every priest stands daily ministering and offering time after time the same sacrifices, which can never take away sins; but he, having offered one sacrifice for sins for all time, sat down at the right hand of God"* (Hebrews 10:11, 12).

So too the Atonement Day sabbath, along with all sabbaths, was fulfilled, taken over and upgraded into a sabbath rest in him – *"Come unto me, all you who are weary and heavy-laden, and I will give you rest"*, *"Come unto me and sabbath"*.[4] It is not that Jesus has destroyed the Law and the Prophets; he interprets them as they were meant to be understood 'in him'. *"For the one who has entered his rest has himself also rested from his works"* (Hebrews 4:10) and if we have been to the one sacrifice of the Lamb of God *"there is no longer any offering for sin"* (Hebrews 10:3, 4, 12, 14, 18).

The writer of Hebrews has rightly understood the revamping of the Day of Atonement in Jesus' teaching in the light of the whole

[4]Compare Matthew 11:28, 29 and Matthew 12:1-14 for the context of these well-known words; here also we see Jesus' understanding of the inadequate and temporary teaching on the nature of animal sacrifice which the prophets had pointed out already, eg. Hosea 6:6, which Jesus now quotes in Matthew 12:7.

11

narrative of Matthew (cf. Matthew 11:25-12:14) even if this particular Old Testament holy day is not mentioned explicitly in this passage. Few Christians would seek to re-introduce the practice of the Day of Atonement now that Christ has died for the sins of the world. However, some Christians may feel a voluntary desire to fast in the New Testament age since Jesus did say, more generally than perhaps for the Day of Atonement, that the time would come when his disciples would spontaneously fast. This would be at a time when he would be taken away from them (Mark 2:20).

The word *"taken away"* implies a violent removal and its use in Isaiah 53:8 in the Septuagint[5] confirms the thought that this is an allusion to the cross. It is the same passage (Mark 2:18-28) where Jesus clearly challenges the old structures of Judaism (old wineskin) as being inadequate to preserve the new wine of the future age, that of the Holy Spirit. He goes on to indicate that the Son of Man is the Lord of the sabbath (v.28) – presumably the Atonement Day sabbath included – to give it its true meaning of ceasing from our own works and thus introducing the rest of grace.

Jesus foresaw the future structure or wineskin of the Church as flexible, not legal and rigid. Sometimes we feast – the Bridegroom is with us by his Spirit; sometimes we fast – he is yet to return. Jesus understood the Day of Atonement with its fasting, sacrifices and sabbath rest in a fresh way. Our conclusion is that he at least hinted, if not advocated, sometimes feasting, sometimes fasting. Putting it another way, fasting was to be a free will response and not a prescribed legal injunction as the Law of Moses taught. Christians are not under the Law as the Jews. This leads us to the second category of Old Testament fast days.

b) The National or Corporate Fast
Esther 4:3 was a spontaneous response to a crisis for God's ancient people (they were threatened with extermination, Esther 3:13), which became a regular fast of Israel (Esther 9:31) even

---

[5]Greek translation of the Old Testament.

though it was not ordained in the Law. Zechariah 8:18-19 tells of four more national corporate fasts on account of disasters which occurred in Israel.

The fourth month fast recalled the month in which the wall of the city of Jerusalem was breached (Jeremiah 39:2); the fifth month fast marked the tragedy of the destruction of the Temple (2 Kings 25:8f); the seventh month had a fast that commemorated the murder of Gedaliah (Jeremiah 41:1f) and the tenth month fast reminded the people of the beginning of the siege of Jerusalem (Jeremiah 39:1). But Zechariah tells us that these non-statutory, voluntary fasts of repentance for Israel were to become feasts: *"Thus says the Lord of hosts: 'the fast of the fourth, the fast of the fifth, the fast of the seventh and the fast of the tenth months will become joy, gladness and cheerful feasts for the house of Judah'"* (Zechariah 8:19).

Perhaps this is the background for Jesus' view of fasting now that the Bridegroom was with them: *"And Jesus said to them, 'While the bridegroom is with them, the attendants of the bridegroom do not fast, do they? So long as they have the bridegroom with them they cannot fast. But the day will come when the bridegroom is taken away from them and then they will fast in that day'"* (Mark 2:19, 20). The Church lives in the overlap of the ages; sometimes we fast, sometimes we feast.

It would seem that in the Old Testament days there was scope and freedom to introduce corporate, recommended and customary fasts as appropriate, and this appears to be our Lord's approach; having fulfilled and filled up the one statutory fast day of Moses by his death, thereby making it redundant, he now allows the freedom of voluntary fasting, both corporate or individual during the time of his presence by the Spirit and yet absent in his body. The Church age needs this flexible wineskin if it is to contain and preserve the Spirit.

c) The Individually Chosen Fast

In the paragraph above this third Old Testament category of fast has been anticipated. It was stated that the corporate fast could appear and disappear in those Old Testament days, but so too

13

individual fasts were appropriate and acceptable: Moses (Deuteronomy 9:18), Elijah (1 Kings 19:8), Daniel (Daniel 10:3) to name but three individuals who undertook such fasts (cf. also Nehemiah 1:4, Ezra 8:23, Esther 4:16, etc). That Jesus followed this Old Testament example of individually chosen fasts should be sufficient to signify a Christian practice. That he never forbade fasting, but assumed that his disciples would fast is a matter that will be examined later. Without further qualification the words concerning his disciples, *"They will fast in that day"* (Mark 2:20), would be quite misleading if it meant disciples of Jesus between the cross and resurrection were to follow this practice but the New Testament saints were never to fast in the New Testament age which was dawning. Clearly the church of the Acts of the Apostles fasted as they felt the need or were guided (Acts 13:1-3, 14:23).

d) Voluntary Regular Fasting

Before we pass on to Jesus' own practice we need to note a fourth category of fast that developed from the Old Testament into Jesus' day. Pharisees in first-century Judaism fasted twice a week (Luke 18:12) and in the parable of the Pharisee and the tax collector Jesus shows one such Pharisee who, having used the Old Testament example of voluntary self-initiated fasting for himself, is now making it into law for every Jew – a legal means of righteousness to find acceptability with God instead of a contrite and desperate plea to God for mercy.

Fasting now can be a means of self-righteousness, a meritorious act, which would exalt the man in his own eyes and probably the eyes of others. Jesus' wonderful story of the quisling, hard-bitten tax collector being right with God while the self-righteous Pharisee was not, despite his fasting, shows the danger element which Jesus highlights with respect to fasting. The second-century Church, which evidently practised regular fasting like the Pharisees, was aware of this danger. Warned by Jesus, they did not advocate, as can be seen in the Didache (a second-century Christian manual on church practice), that the church members should not fast on Mondays and Thursdays like the hypocrites – for example the Pharisee in Jesus' story – but rather on Wednesdays and Fridays! How close this comes to a new Christianised legalism is for us each to judge.

Individual Christians must be exercised by and engage in fasting if our discipleship is serious, but it is to be done with Jesus' warning that the discipline of a disciple is never to usurp the devotion it is meant to express and quicken. A man may glory in his wife, and bring home thousands of presents to develop and express his love and communion with her, giving himself to her in his gifts. Another man may glory in his ideal of loving, measuring his devotion to his wife by the number of gifts he makes but his admiration is of himself, and of his ideal of himself as a great lover, not his delight in his wife for her own sake. So Jesus would get hold of us through our fasting, and not simply have us get hold of our fasting as a meritorious gift.

2. Jesus

Jesus has been seen in his relationship to the Old Testament and its teaching which he came not to dissolve but to complete. He has been seen in particular in relationship to the Old Testament fasting which as a Jew he inherited and is seen to embody, beautify and excel. But what further light does he shine on to the practice for us to emulate and enjoy?

The New Testament word for fasting *nēsteia* literally means "not eating". The public ministry of our Lord was introduced after his baptism, anointing of the Spirit and temptation (Matthew 3:13-4:17). This last event had a duration of forty days and was accompanied by fasting. The trial and presumably the fasting was prompted by the Holy Spirit and therefore must be seen not so much as self-imposed (and of course not inflicted on Jesus by some corporate societal pressure) but as a free following of the Spirit. Both the freedom and Holy Spirit's guidance are seen in Jesus, and stand out at the head of the New Testament church age as characteristic of all that we do in obedience to God, including fasting which this passage directly highlights.

Of course there is a unique element for Jesus in this great event

15

which should not be overlooked. Jesus reflects and takes up into himself the experience of the only two other great persons who also fasted forty days, Moses (possibly on 2 occasions, Deuteronomy 9:9 and 18), and Elijah (1 Kings 19:8): Moses, the representative of the Law who fasted for forty days at the beginning of Israel's history, and Elijah who represented the prophets. The last words of the Old Testament in Malachi 4:4-6 show that the influence, if not the presence of these two was to reappear at the end of the age: *"Remember the law of Moses my servant, even the statutes and ordinances which I commanded him in Horeb for all Israel. Behold, I am going to send you Elijah the prophet before the coming of the great and terrible day of the Lord. And he will restore the hearts of the fathers to their children and the hearts of the children to their fathers, lest I come and smite the land with a curse."* These verses also show that Elijah was destined to share with Moses an influence on the end-time by coming to turn the hearts of the fathers back to the children and the children to the fathers.

Jesus is presented in conjunction with these mentors of Israel, not just in sharing in their experience of a forty-day fast, but this time on the Mount of Transfiguration where they point to Jesus as the fulfilment of all the Law and Prophets, prophecies and ministries. This is confirmed by God's words, *"This is my Son, hear him."*

Whatever role Moses and Elijah were destined to play in the inauguration of the day of Jesus, will only be seen in the light of Jesus himself (Matthew 11:11-14, Luke 1:17). All that they were before God is taken over and caught up into the Son of God (Hebrews 1:1, 2). So there is a distinctive which belongs to the only recorded fast of Jesus: just as Moses and Elijah introduced the Law and the Prophets, so now the new age of Jesus and the Spirit is introduced in a similar way. All that Moses and Elijah stood for is recycled and they are superseded by the Son of God (Deuteronomy 18:15). Forty days of prayer is a fitting symbol and a powerful spiritual experience with which to introduce the new age of the Kingdom and its people.

While accepting that for Jesus this forty-day fast has distinct personal connotations, nevertheless it may be said that its

16

example for those of us who are his body today is still relevant.

Two things stand out. First the conflict through which Jesus conquered the devil, assisted as it was by fasting, must stand as an example for those of us who follow him. We follow him in his baptism (Luke 3:21), we follow him in receiving the Spirit (Luke 3:22), we follow him into ministry (Luke 3:23). It seems unlikely, since we are sons and daughters of God who are led of the Spirit (Romans 8:14), that we will not at times be led by the Spirit to encounter and defeat the enemy, or at least his underlings, in a similar way (Ephesians 6:12). Perhaps at the beginning of a public ministry it would be an ideal practice for his followers, as it was for their Master, to so engage the enemy. Paul, however, indicates such a battle will continue throughout our fight of faith as the remark of Luke 4:13 *("And when the devil had finished every temptation, he departed from him until an opportune time")* points to the fact that it was an ongoing battle for Jesus. That the devil has to depart throughout our ministry for times and seasons if we resist him is assured and is a relief from battle, but the war will not cease throughout our ministry. Fasting will clearly be a part of our spiritual warfare as it was with Jesus.

Secondly, a factor closely associated with the equipment we need for service is the strength of character which is developed through fasting. Fasting appears to be a part of our preparation for service in the developing of our character as well as defeating Satan. Clearly Jesus' faith was perfected in this time since the devil repeatedly attacked his Sonship. *"If you are the Son of God."* So our faith and sonship will be refined in fasting and fighting.

The Sermon on the Mount (Matthew 5-7) is explicitly given in the context of the subject of a righteousness that exceeds that of the scribes and Pharisees (Matthew 5:20). To be right with God of course requires a righteousness which none of us has apart from grace *"because by the works of the Law no flesh will be justified in his sight; for through the Law comes the knowledge of sin. But now apart from the Law the righteousness of God has been made manifest, being witnessed by the Law and the Prophets, even the righteousness of God through faith in Jesus Christ for all those who believe;"* (Romans 3:20-2).

Nevertheless, as vital as that God-given righteousness is, Jesus is not referring in the first place to the righteousness which is God's in this sermon, but to an integrity in our living which is not merely skin deep, but of the heart (*"But I say to you that everyone who is angry with is brother shall be guilty before the course; ...But I say to you that everyone who looks on a woman to lust for her has committed adultery already with her in his heart"* Matthew 5:22, 28) and which is not for hypocritical display to others, but in secret when only God is around (*"...and your Father who sees in secret will repay you"* Matthew 6:2, 6, 16). Jesus is speaking of a righteousness which is not only in the talk of righteousness and so exhausts its ability to act but actually a righteousness which does the will of God (Matthew 7:21).

It is in this context that Jesus introduces his explicit teaching on fasting (Matthew 6:16-18). He accepts the three great disciplines of Judaism: prayer, giving and fasting and expounds each, not with the assumption that since he has come they will be abandoned, but that any follower of his will practise them. In fact it is apparently unthinkable that they would not do so. For instance, *"when you fast..."* (v.16) takes it for granted that any serious disciple will fast as equally as it is meaningless in this chapter to be a worshipper of God or a disciple of Jesus if you do not pray and give.

Again, having established the necessity of fasting Jesus gives its context – secrecy; it is to be seen by Father not by men (v.18). Just as there is the necessity of secrecy in prayer (v.6) and in giving (v.4), so too with fasting. Of course there needs to be allowed a certain freedom of interpretation for secrecy in prayer, giving and fasting. For instance, public prayer and group prayer and the gathering together of offerings publicly are not violating what Jesus is saying here. So too, over-literal legalism concerning the secrecy of fasting is not what is intended. It is rather that fasting is not something for public display, although at times there may be public calls for such and bodies of believers doing it together would acknowledge to each other that they are fasting, as in Acts: 13 1-3.

Rather, Jesus is tackling the motivation: it is for Father. It is not to parade our piety and let others be impressed by our devotion and sacrifice but rather our fasting is to impress God, our clearing the ground for him. Love, truth, righteousness and the disciplines must have their returns in a universe produced by a moral God. Such will inevitably have their rewards, as Jesus says, but not in worldly coinage. If any of the disciplines, and fasting in particular, are engaged in for the world's adulation, that is the return they will receive. "You've had it" could be the paraphrase of verse 16 but our Father who sees in secret searches the heart that we may fast unto him alone.

It is interesting to note that the individual intimacy with the Father that Jesus is here advocating, is reinforced by his 'singular' use of the word *your* Father in verses 4, 6 and 18. In the Authorised Version this is rendered "thy Father"; such a translation reminds us that this is the only place in the Gospels where our individual relationship as opposed to our corporate relationship with Father is emphasised in such a way by Jesus. Fasting, generally speaking, like prayer and giving, is a lover's secret held between each individual man and woman and his or her God. Self-display and self-righteousness have no place in the intimacy of sons and daughters of God with their Father.

Finally Jesus teaches, with an eye to the secrecy already discussed, that the New Testament fasting is already turning to feasting. Old Testament religious clothes, garments of mourning and dust of death *"sackcloth and ashes"* (Matthew 6:16), are already gone – we are fasting for the feasting, eating the spiritual bread of the coming kingdom, or the *"bread of the morrow"*, as the Lord's prayer strictly calls it (Matthew 6:11). Already the future feasting being eaten now precludes the total renunciation of the present. We have to fast with joy in anticipation of the future, anointing our heads and washing our faces (v.17). No one but God is to see our self-denial for we represent the age to come and the Messianic Banquet (Luke 14:15).

It was in this manner that Jesus defended his disciples when they were accused of not fasting (Matthew 9:14ff). The Pharisees and John the Baptist's disciples fasting – "anyone with religious aspirations fasted" is the implication and the criticism. Already it has been noted that there is a tension in Jesus' answer *"how can they fast when the Bridegroom is with them?"*; no one should fast while a feast is on the table. However, Jesus will be taken away by violent death, then they will spontaneously fast, but for how long? Surely the resurrection and Pentecost reverse their mourning and sadness and must they not now feast again?

The flexible wineskin (Matthew 9:17) is the structure of the new people of God. As we have seen earlier, although a certain amount of license was given for new feasts and fasts for the old people, the feast of the Day of Atonement stood firm as a law for everyone as indeed did the command to come up to the place that God would choose, namely Jerusalem, and rejoice. Presumably 'rejoice' was a command whether you felt like it or not.

This structure of Israel was an inelastic, inflexible structure of law and legalism necessary for a people of the Old Testament age, but inappropriate for a people with the Pentecostal Spirit. Now the time had come when the promised Spirit was poured out on all flesh and sons and daughters prophesied, therefore a new wineskin was necessary for this intoxicating refreshing. The kingdom of justice, joy and peace in the Holy Spirit is now with us (Romans 14:17) but it is *still* coming. The judgement had passed (John 5:24) but Jesus would still gather the nations for a final verdict on their lives (Matthew 25:31f). The deaf hear, the lame walk, the dead are raised but until the resurrection has arrived, the whole of the kingdom will not be here. The kingdom is now but not yet, it has come but it is still coming, it is still to be prayed for while it is yet in our midst.

In the same vein, the flexible wineskin of the church will include both feasting and fasting. Such seems to be the Lord's defence of his disciples. No legalised fasting is instituted but voluntary, spontaneous exercising led by the Spirit of God will mean sometimes feasting, sometimes fasting, sometimes drinking, sometimes thirsting. Jesus had said somewhat enigmatically at the last supper (Matthew 26:29): *"I will not drink of this fruit of the vine from now on till the day when I drink it new with you in my Father's kingdom."*

Did he mean that he is with us now as we drink at the Lord's table or did he refer to a future date at the Marriage Supper of the Lamb? Is it the wine of the Spirit that we now find moving our hearts or will it be at the Messianic Banquet? Equally we pass through this current scene, feasting and fasting. Of course the best wine is kept till last (John 2:10)!

Jesus once said that *"my meat is to do the will of him who sent me and to accomplish His work"* (John 4:31-4). Perhaps we feast because we do the work of him who sends us, but then we do not do it completely and so we mourn in our imperfection and inadequacy in order that we might find more grace to enjoy more completely doing His will.

3. New Testament Church

Thirdly we must ask, how did the church of the Acts of the Apostles and the Letters understand and practice by the Spirit of Jesus our Lord's teaching on fasting? In the best Greek text there are at least ten verses to consider.

a) Acts 9:9
Paul spontaneously fasts in repentance.

b) Acts 13:2
It seems normal for the church leaders of Antioch and presumably elsewhere, to fast for ministry to the Lord and to receive His guidance.

c) Acts 13:3
Again it seems normal for the church to fast and pray in sending forth their missionaries.

d) Acts 14:23
Praying and fasting accompanies the choice and public appointment of church leaders – it should be assumed that the church here at Pisidian Antioch also joined in the prayer and fasting.

e) 2 Corinthians 6:5 and (f) 2 Corinthians 11:27
These occurrences have been questioned as to whether they mean fasting, but the list of spiritual values in 2 Corinthians 6:6 indicates that 2 Corinthians 6:5 may be understood as fasting to

God while 2 Corinthians 11:27 must mean fasting to God, else it merely is a repeat of what has already been said earlier in the verse and is redundant (cf. *IVP Dictionary* article referred to earlier).

g) Acts 1:14
Given the fact that the quotation from Joel 2:28-32 (Acts 2:16-21) follows very soon after this verse, it is possible that the praying of the 120 leading up to Pentecost was shaped by earlier verses in Joel (1:14, 2:12, 15-20), and was accompanied as these verses indicate, by fasting. Acts 1:14 does emphasise with the definite article "*the* prayer". Perhaps it was the Joel prayer?

h) 1 Corinthians 8:13 and (i) Romans 14:21
Appear to be a partial fast for a weak brother.

j) 1 Timothy 4:3-4
This is a negative reference warning about asceticism which glorifies the flesh as Paul also says in Colossians 2:23: *"These are matters which, to be sure, have the appearance of wisdom in self-made religion and self-abasement and severe treatment of the body, but are of no value against fleshly indulgence."* However the warning would have little value unless the practice of fasting was accepted as Christian in the fellowship of believers.

These ten references indicate that in the post-Pentecostal church fasting was accepted and practised as Jesus had taught in the Gospels, or indeed that this is how they understood Jesus to have taught in the Gospels and were now putting into practice. Participation in fasting did not require much exhortation or instruction because it was so generally accepted as a discipline for Christians. Therefore it appears only incidentally and infrequently in the Acts and the Letters.

2

The Purpose of Fasting

The reasons for which men and women fast might be thought discoverable by unearthing the origin of this practice. However, the ancient roots to religious fasting, which occurs in most religions and in most parts of the world, are lost in obscurity. Reasons for certain more recent types of fasting such as Gandhi's fast, or an IRA hunger striker in prison are more readily discernible. They are used for political pressure and protest against social injustices. Such reasons might evoke admiration, but for a Christian they are morally questionable. This is because they are a threat to one's own life with a view to coercing action in one's opponents in order that they may do your will. This is a somewhat dubious motivation for a Christian fast. However, hunger lunches and abstention from luxury foods or all foods in order to identify with the hungry and raise relief for the poor, are very Christlike and would fall into the category of Isaiah 58:6-7: *"Is this not the fast which I choose, to loosen the bonds of wickedness, to undo the bands of the yoke, and to let the oppressed go free, and break every yoke? Is it not to divide your bread with the hungry, and bring the homeless poor into the house; when you see the naked, to cover him; and not to hide yourself from your own flesh?"*

Isaiah goes further to show that such fasting from material things will also lead to spiritual expansion and an effective prayer life.

> *"Then your light will break out like the dawn, And your recovery will speedily spring forth; and your righteousness will go before you; the glory of the Lord will be your rearguard. Then you will call, and the Lord will answer; you will cry, and he will say, 'Here I am.' If you remove the yoke*

from your midst, the pointing of the finger, and speaking wickedness, and if you give yourself to the hungry, and satisfy the desire of the afflicted, then your light will rise in darkness, and your gloom will become like midday. And the Lord will continually guide you, and satisfy your desire in scorched places, and give strength to your bones; and you will be like a watered garden, and like a spring of water whose waters do not fail. And those from among you will rebuild the ancient ruins; you will raise up the age-old foundations; and you will be called the repairer of the breach, the restorer of the streets in which to dwell."

(Isaiah 58: 8-12)

Although it has been suggested that care for the hungry is a modern reason for fasting, Isaiah 58 indicates it was the concern of the eighth century BC prophets, while in 128 AD Aristides reported to the Emperor Hadrian that the Christians fasted two or three days and gave the food they saved to the poor.

Sometimes fasting is promoted in order that the body may be toned up and function more efficiently. Health regimes are sometimes the province of weight-watchers and body worshippers, but to have a healthy, well-kept temple for the Holy Spirit is a proper aspiration for a practising Christian. Paul might be referring to fasting amongst other things when he says that he buffets his body in 1 Corinthians 9:27. This, of course, is only three chapters after 1 Corinthians 6:19 and 20 where he refers to the body as the temple of the Holy Spirit. To have a toned-up and more readily disciplined body is a wise thing and a very acceptable instrument to offer to the Lord's service.

Such reasons for specific and more specialised fastings are readily grasped. However it is necessary to investigate the biblical reasons for fasting in a more comprehensive way. Perhaps the original motivation and therefore understanding for fasting, came from the natural abstention from food at the time of bereavement or grief. A person's lack of appetite for the basic physical pleasures of well-being is known in such times. Abstention from sexual pleasure which is chosen for spiritual reasons as in Exodus 19:15 and 1 Corinthians 7:4-6 also makes sense if this natural reaction to grief lies at the basis of fasting. Just as fasting from food is linked with prayer in the Scriptures so is fasting from sexual activity between a husband and wife (*"by agreement, for a time"*, 1 Corinthians 7:5). So the experience associated with mourning could possibly lie at the root of a more deliberate and self-chosen fast made for other and spiritual reasons. The Scriptures would seem to concur with this in identifying mourning in bereavement and then later mourning over sin with the practice of fasting. 1 Samuel 31:13, 2 Samuel 1:12, 3:35, 1 Chronicles 10:12 relate fasting to mourning over Saul's and Jonathan's deaths and the later death of their general Abner, while in Daniel 6:18 Darius abstains from food during the night when he thought Daniel had been destroyed in the lions' den. Grief from bereavement and from anger, which as Jonathan demonstrates in 1 Samuel 20:34, 28:20 are sometimes associated, are spontaneously expressed with fasting. This automatic, understandable human response to mourning and grief would seem to lie at the roots of the practice of fasting in relationship to God. Mourning over sin and the necessary repentance to God result in fasting as seen in Ezra 9:5, 10:6 (*"Ezra did not eat bread nor drink water for he was mourning over the unfaithfulness of the exiles"*) Leviticus 16:29-31, and Matthew 5:4.

If human experience and Scripture's confirmation give such a rationale for fasting, in what further ways do the Scriptures give believers more specific reasons for choosing this practice? It is the intention of this booklet to refer to every Scripture directly related to fasting, and also to verses which appear to have a bearing on the subject, even if only barely related. Only in this way can we achieve a comprehensive explanation of our subject. As this could result in a rather daunting, if not exhausting list of Scriptures, these verses have been categorised into three lists of seven items each. The three categories are: 1. Commitment; 2. Need; 3. Breakthrough. Each of the twenty-one purposes for fasting will have some verses and the minimum of comment. The verses will demonstrate the reasons given by the Bible for fasting, but also will enable the reader to meditate and consider further, thereby gaining deeper insights as to why God has given us this discipline.

1. Commitment

a) Determination to complete a task
(Genesis 24:33, 1 Samuel 14:24-30, Acts 23:12-21, 27:21-33)

In some of these cases it was undoubtedly wrong to fast. For instance, when the intention was to do evil, as with those planning to kill Paul, or Saul trying to take God's glory to himself. Sometimes it was necessary, as with the sailors in Paul's experience of shipwreck, in order to keep the ship afloat. Nonetheless Abraham's servant put aside eating to speed the fulfilment of his duty; his fasting hastened his obedience.

b) Strength in worship
(Leviticus 23:14, Esther 9:31, Acts 13:2)

Fasting had to precede the wave offering (Leviticus 23:14). This took place on the very day which was to become the day of Jesus' resurrection as foreseen by God in Leviticus. Spiritual energy is required for resurrection as it is indeed for resurrection worship – that is by our exaltation and offering up the living Christ to the Father by our praise, as is foreshadowed in the wave offering. The fasting that was done naturally when Jesus was in the grave, now is undertaken in order to present Christ to God in worship. Esther fasts in order to ordain a celebration; for this task she requires spiritual energy. And for the leaders of the church in Antioch to serve, that is, to minister to the Lord, they needed the strength for such a tremendous calling and privilege which comes through fasting. Ministering to the Lord is an honour beyond description so that we are able to serve God and give him pleasure by our worship. No wonder at times they felt it necessary to fast for this great occupation.

c) Confirmation of an oath
(Numbers 6:1-4, 1 Kings 13:8-24, Acts 23:12-21)

The Nazarite in Numbers 6, the young prophet of 1 Kings, and the evil men vowing to assassinate Paul all needed to confirm their commitment in the oaths and vows they took. Fasting was the means to which they resorted. Fasting, then, opens us up to the spiritual world (good or evil), and facilitates the infusion of spiritual energy and life.

d) Self-discipline
(2 Samuel 11:11, 1 Kings 17:6, 14-16, Daniel 1:12-16,
Matthew 11:18, 19, Luke 7:33, 34, 1 Corinthians 9:27)
In 2 Samuel Uriah very commendably fasts from feasting and
enjoying his wife while his fellow-soldiers are still in the field of
battle. This shows the discipline of a hardened soldier, but
possibly is also an implied criticism of David with maybe a hint
of suspicion of the king's sudden interest in his welfare, since
David had seduced his wife Bathsheba. In 1 Kings, Elijah eats
only what God sends, then the woman sacrifices her food and is
blessed. These are disciplined approaches to obedience – *"Give
and it shall be given to you"* (Luke 6:38). Daniel and his friends
fast from luxuries in order to feel free from the king.

Such restraints give us liberty in the decisions that we make,
uninfluenced by any strings that might be pulling us by those who
are our benefactors or superiors. To indulge in the provision of the
patron can result in compromise. John the Baptist, in the verses
from Matthew was accused of being demonised because he
fasted. Jesus seemed less ascetic and freer in his approach to the
good things of life but was also attacked by the religious, possibly
brandishing Deuteronomy 21:20, 21: *"and they shall say to the
elders of his city, 'This son of ours is stubborn and rebellious, he
will not obey us, he is a glutton and a drunkard.' Then all the men
of his city shall stone him to death; so you shall remove the evil
from your midst, and all Israel shall hear of it and fear."*

Sometimes to be a friend of sinners requires fasting from the
world's opinion and expectancy of a man or woman of God. Each
of us must be guided by the Spirit as to the form and the time of
fasting – this is discipline also. Perhaps Paul in 1 Corinthians 9:27
is referring to fasting amongst other things when he speaks of
making his body serve him and not he serve his body.

e) Mourning sin
(Ezra 9:5, 10:1, 6, Matthew 5:4)
Ezra's mourning over Israel's sin is very deep and is expressed by
fasting, while Jesus' beatitude in the sermon on the mount,

27

though not mentioning fasting or sin, is undoubtedly to be understood as involving the Old Testament background from which he spoke (Matthew 5:17-18), even though he was deepening it.

f) Preparing for the Day of the Lord – the coming of the Spirit
(Joel 1:14, 15, 2:1, 12-17)

Both these chapters of Joel are concerned with God's judgement which was to be administered on the Day of the Lord. Fasting from food and marriage enjoyment are called for so that the Lord might avert his judgement. This judgement is seen earlier in a hoard of locusts bringing a famine in their devastating wake. However, there is hope in Joel's fast. *"Who knows, perhaps God will relent and turn his judgement into a blessing and leave enough harvest for a grain offering and a drink offering for himself"*, (2:14). Indeed God does relent and pours out his rain (2:23) which typifies the pouring out of his Spirit (2:28). We can only speculate, but it seems very reasonable to assume in the light of Joel being quoted in Acts 2 that the prayer of Acts 1:14[6] included fasting and was inspired by Joel 1 and 2.

Many outpourings of the Spirit have been preceded by prayer and fasting, and so prayer and fasting should precede world evangelisation and the return of Jesus which is to be seen as the Day of the Lord. The preaching of the good news in all the world in order that the end might come (Matthew 24:14) will be more surely accomplished by a church committed to prayer and to fasting.

g) Helping weaker brothers
(1 Corinthians 8:13, Romans 14:21)

Paul shows us how to lovingly restrain ourselves in our eating and drinking in order to help brothers and sisters with weaker consciences.

Not only does fasting reinforce our commitment, but it alleviates our needs:-

[6]The definite article precedes the word "prayer" so it could be that an even more definite and specific prayer was being prayed: *"the prayer"* rather than just "prayer" in general.

2. Need

a) Reception of understanding or revelation
(Exodus 34:28, Luke 2:37, 38, Acts 9:9-12, Daniel 10:1-3)
The apostle Paul prayed for the Ephesians that they might receive the Spirit of wisdom and revelation in the full knowledge of Christ (Ephesians 1:17). Fasting with prayer opens up the human spirit to the Holy Spirit, who leads us into all truth (John 16:13, 14). Moses, in order to receive the Law, Anna, to see God's redemption (that is Jesus), Paul and Daniel, along with many others, fasted to see and to understand God's heart, truth and ways.

b) Repentance for forgiveness
(Leviticus 16:29-31, 23:27-36, Numbers 29:7, Jeremiah 36:6-9)
Jeremiah sends Baruch to read the words of the Lord to the people in the hope that they might repent. The day this is to be done in the temple courts is a fast day to give reality and strength to their repentance. If that day was the one day that God had commanded people to fast, as in the Law of Moses, then it would have been the Day of Atonement which is the subject of the three other passages of Scripture (cf. Acts 27:9). Sacrifices were made on that day for sin and for a sweet aroma to the Lord. The scapegoat also was presented to the Lord and sent into the wilderness, carrying all the sins of the people while another goat was 'made sin' and offered to the Lord.

These offerings show that repentance itself was not adequate for forgiveness, but sacrifices, anticipating the sacrifice of Christ, the Son of God, were the ground of God's atonement; whereas repentance was the means for Israel's receptivity of that right relationship. The repentance commanded each year by God was to be expressed in fasting. First, there was fasting from food which humbled the people and drained away self-sufficiency with its arrogance and unbelief. Then, accompanying this fasting, there was a fasting from work, it was a sabbath. This latter fasting helped Israel to cease from its own works and enter into the rest of faith (Hebrews 4:10). Fasting helps men and women to lose their self-sufficiency and pride casting them in faith on God, and through the sacrifice of Jesus, to be assured of God's forgiveness and of their own acceptance by him.

c) Turning failure into victory
(Judges 20:26ff)
When Israel sought to judge and purge the sin of the Benjaminites they twice failed. Therefore they resorted to prayer and fasting, turning their failure into success on the third attempt. Fasting leads to victory in areas of our lives in which we are weak.

d) Protection
(Ezra 8:21-3, Esther 4:16)
Ezra sought protection from God for the returning exiles, and Esther asked others to join her in fasting for her safe-keeping when she had an audience with the king. To request an audience with the king without being first invited was to risk the penalty of death. Protection from men and women as indeed from the evil forces which lie behind them, is received through fasting.

e) Renewal
(Daniel 9:3, Nehemiah 1:4, 9:1)
Nehemiah fasted and later the people joined him for the renewal of the devastated city of Jerusalem and the people of God. The signed agreement of the people (Nehemiah 9:38) was virtually a renewing of the covenant and was inspired by the fasting at the beginning of the same chapter. Daniel's fast was initiated by his desire for the renewal of Israel also. The seventy years of exile prophesied by Jeremiah were ending, but not with the desired renewal of spiritual life for which many had hoped. Daniel's prayer, fasting and confession of the people's sin was met with an angelic visitation revealing that the renewal of God's purposes in Israel was not only in relation to a seventy year period, but for seventy times seven years into the future.

f) Supernatural strength
(1 Kings 19:8, Deuteronomy 9:9)
Both Moses and Elijah were sustained supernaturally for forty days and nights going without water as well as food. Such a fast without water would be impossible naturally. However, spiritual

power sustained them in their fast and presumably was received on the basis of their fasting.

g) Healing of body and spirit
(1 Samuel 1:1-7, Psalm 35:13, 14, 107:1-20, 109:4)
Hannah's infertility was healed after fasting. The Psalms have many allusions to healing of the body and spirit, but at least these three references connect fasting to the prayer for healing. David prayed, mourned and fasted for his enemies when they were sick, and sinners spontaneously fast when sick, till God sends his word and heals. Psalm 109 is a Messianic psalm quoted in the New Testament to explain Judas' betrayal of Jesus (Acts 1:20). It is especially interesting on at least three accounts for it appears that a great amount of the suffering is in the spirit. Secondly, that it was caused largely by cursing or evil speaking (vv. 2, 3, 4, 17, 18, 19, 20, 28, 29). The response to this affliction is first prayer (v.4), then fasting (v.24). Thirdly, however, these two aspects are probably expected to be understood as one entity in that verse 4 is literally translated *"I am prayer"*. The whole being of the psalmist and indeed of our Lord was in itself an appeal to God, a calling on God, a prayer to God for deliverance. Fasting is just this: it offers prayers to God, not just by lifting up holy hands which are a part of our body (1 Timothy 2:8), but presenting the whole body as both a vehicle for prayer and indeed prayer itself to the Lord.

3. Breakthrough

a) Averting God's wrath
(Deuteronomy 9:18-20, 2 Samuel 12:21-3, 1 Kings 13:8-24)
Moses prayed and fasted and God's wrath was averted from Israel and Aaron; David prayed and fasted, but the prophesied death of David's child was not however averted. But the fasting was David's only possible recourse if he were to halt the judgement. The strange yet challenging story of the old and young prophets obviously suggests that, if the young prophet had continued to fast, he would have avoided God's judgement; but in this case the judgement itself was in relation to the breaking of the fast and

was not on account of seeking something else to which fasting had been the response.

b) Seeking divine intervention
(1 Samuel 7:6, 2 Chronicles 20:3, Esther 4:3)
When Israel was dominated by the Philistines Samuel led the people to reject false idolatry, to repent and to fast for deliverance (1 Samuel 7:1-6) which came through God's intervention with a thunderstorm (v.10, compare Hannah's prophecy in 1 Samuel 2:10). Jehoshaphat commanded a fast throughout Judah; then he led, it seems, the whole of the inhabitants of Jerusalem on a march into the wilderness together with the army and singers. The conjunction of faith, obedience, worship, prayer and fasting led to God taking charge of the battle. *"The battle is not yours but God's"* (2 Chronicles 20:15) and the three enemies, Moab, Ammon and Edom destroyed each other (v.22).

The people in the days of Esther immediately fasted when they heard of their ordained destruction. Esther joined them and God intervened with deliverance in the most marvellous way as the book of Esther tells. Fasting was the means God used to get involved with the affairs of government.

c) Changing God's mind
(Exodus 32:14, Psalm 106:23, Jonah 3:5, 9, 10)
Contrary to popular opinion God can and does change his mind. Exodus 32:14 clearly shows this while Moses was praying and fasting for Israel (Psalm 106:23). Abraham changed God's mind concerning the destruction of Sodom while he prayed down the number of people necessary to be in righteous agreement or solidarity of the city (see Genesis 18:16ff and also Amos 7:1-9, Jeremiah 26:3, 36:3, 1 Samuel 15:35). Nineveh in the days of Jonah repented with fasting and so God changed his mind also, much to Jonah's embarrassment (Jonah 4).

d) Seeking God's presence
(Psalms 42, 43)
God has promised to be in the midst of his people (Matthew 18:20) and worship is the ethos of his presence, *"The Lord*

inhabits the praises of Israel" (Psalm 22:3). Often when his presence seems diminished or distanced fasting should be resorted to in order to recover the sense of divine presence. Psalms 42 and 43 speak of just that longing. Psalm 42:3 indicates fasting was the cry for the return of God's face (v.5) while 43:2 in the light of 42:9 indicates that food was abstained from while the return of God's face was sought.

e) Appointment of elders
(Acts 14:23)
This and matters of like importance in which God's mind is needed in the church, should be sought with fasting and prayer.

f) Sending of missionaries
(Acts 13:1-3)
The whole operation of the church, identifying and releasing Barnabas and Paul as apostles sent to extend the gospel – *"the work to which I have called them"* – was born and nurtured in prayer and fasting. The leaders, the church and the apostles all fasted for this great commissioning. How much more should we be fasting in the sending out of our missionaries today?

g) World evangelisation
(Zechariah 7:5, 8:18-23)
It might appear strange to refer to this Old Testament book of Zechariah for verses about world evangelisation. However, it should not be forgotten that the Old Testament was the New Testament church's Bible when interpreted by the Holy Spirit in the light of the *kerygma* (that is, the verbal proclamation of Jesus' birth, life, death, resurrection, ascension, giving of his Spirit and coming again).

So these Old Testament verses along with all of God's Old Testament truth were written for us (*"Now these things happened to them as an example, and they were written for our instruction, upon whom the ends of the ages have come"* 1 Corinthians 10:11).

Much fasting had been introduced throughout the Babylonian exile of Israel in the sixth century BC. This was over and above the one required Mosaic fast of the Day of Atonement; four others had been instituted to commemorate with repentance the disasters that fell on Jerusalem, the temple and the people of God. The fasts were held in the fourth, fifth, seventh and tenth months. It was the fourth year of King Darius (Zechariah 7:1), the exiles had been returning and captivity was over, *"Should we continue to keep these fasts?"* is the obvious current issue for pious Jews (Zechariah 7:3-5). Zechariah's reply is not direct; he first challenges the returned exiles to ask themselves whether their fasts were to God or for their own selfish interest. Indeed had they learnt from the warnings of the former prophets? However, he continues by stating that the four fasts will become joy, gladness and cheerful feasts and that

> *Thus says the Lord of hosts, 'It will yet be that peoples will come, even the inhabitants of many cities. And the inhabitants of one will go to another saying, "Let us go at once to entreat the favour of the Lord, and to seek the Lord of hosts; I will also go." So many peoples and mighty nations will come to seek the Lord of hosts in Jerusalem and to entreat the favour of the Lord. Thus says the Lord of hosts, 'In those days ten men from all nations will grasp the garment of a Jew saying "Let us go with you, for we have heard that God is with you."'* (Zechariah 8:20-23)

That this is happening more and more in the church of all true Jews, that is those whose circumcision is of the heart by the Spirit and whose praise (Jewishness) is of God, is an evident fact of the current state of world evangelisation.[7] Peoples from more nations than ever before are coming to Christ through his Church and his people as they come saying "God is with you".[8]

---

[7] *"But he is a Jew who is one inwardly; and circumcision is that which is of the heart, by the Spirit, not by the letter; and his praise is not from men, but from God."* (Romans 2:29)

[8] *"But if all prophesy, and an unbeliever or an ungifted man enters, he is convicted by all, he is called to account by all; the secrets of his heart are disclosed and so he will fall on his face and worship God, declaring that God is certainly among you."* (1 Corinthians 14:25)

Now what is still left open by the prophet is whether the nations will come to the heavenly Jerusalem (Galatians 4:26) through a fasting church which turns to celebration through their coming, or by a feasting church whose celebrations and joy attract the Gentiles. It is suggested that the question is deliberately left open owing to the nature of the Church age being both fasting and feasting as seen in Mark 2:18-20 and the practice of the early church being both fasting (Acts 13:1-3) and feasting (Acts 2:46). In Acts 13:1-3 fasting is associated clearly with the beginning of a conscious programme for winning the Gentiles, that is world mission; this should therefore encourage us to fast for the success of world mission and to look for its fulfilment after so long a period of the church's self-indulgence and consequent ignoring of the great commission. Fasting for world mission is perhaps a challenge for this current time.

3

Types of
Fasting

Before listing and describing different kinds of fast and also noting some spiritual dangers associated with this discipline it would be good to summarise succinctly the previous chapter.

Its source is almost certainly to be found in the normal abstention from this world's pleasures at the time of bereavement.

Its essence is therefore:

a) *mourning*, particularly over sin (Matthew 5:4, 9:15, Mark 2:19).

b) *petition*, as human frailty and dependence on God are exposed and expressed, appealing to God for help, since without him there is no hope. Even without prayer, fasting appeals to God: the unspoken message is that to receive God's will and intervention is more important than to receive food.

c) *humility* (Psalm 35:13) is a fundamental strand of the nature of fasting; it says in effect "I deserve nothing". One Hebrew word for fasting means *'to humble oneself'* as seen in Leviticus 16:29-31 (cf. also Jeremiah 36:6-9).

d) *repentance*, for instance in Joel 2:12-13, is closely related to mourning over sin but more generally is calling on God to purge and change the mind and direction. It says "Here I am with no strength to oppose or rebel." This kind of fasting is submission to God.

Its fruit is:

a) *the intensifying* of the impact made by prayer. This impact is both inward and outward. Inwardly, there is in the one praying the personal benefit of discipline in concentrating and focusing his or her prayer; outwardly there is the benefit of greater spiritual power being released into the external situations being addressed through fasting.

b) *the asserting* of the primacy of the spiritual over the physical and material. Rather than the body (1 Corinthians 9:26, 27) and the carnal dominating our existence, the spirit and consequently the Holy Spirit are given freedom to reign (cf. Galatians 5:16, 17).

c) *the purifying* of the body and spirit. If cleansing out the waste products tones up the body to be a temple fit for the Holy Spirit, it also drains away unbelief, opening up more spiritual insight (Ephesians 1:17), alerting the spirit to be more aware of the world forces of darkness and spiritual forces of wickedness (Ephesians 6:12).

d) *the changing* of us. It exposes us to God, giving God the appeal and commission to change us to what he wills and to use us in a more dynamic way.

Its dangers, although not mentioned in this chapter, have been referred to in chapter one so it is fitting to look at this aspect in this summary. Isaiah 58 and Zechariah 7 in the Old Testament and Matthew 6:16 and 1 Timothy 4:3 in the New Testament are warnings concerning the use of fasting. In essence the dangers are hypocrisy and self righteousness.

Isaiah 58 is a scathing chapter on the religiosity which parades its false sanctity and yet is exploiting employees and oppressing the poor while disregarding the need of the hungry and the homeless. It is a passage to which Jesus alluded in his parables and teachings. The parable of the sheep and goats (Matthew 25) reflects verse 7. The last phrase of verse 7, *"hide yourself from your own flesh"*, is a description of the rich man's relationship to Lazarus in the well-known story of Luke 16:19-31.

No doubt Jesus would have had Isaiah 58 in mind when he summed up the parable saying that if the rich man had the Law and the prophets, then nothing more could be given to him in order to activate his social conscience. It must be said, however, that Isaiah 58 is not a passage from which to reject fasting as such, but one that says fasting for one's own interest instead of for God's and exhibiting at the same time a total lack of social conscience and social practice will bring God's condemnation. The complaint of verse 3a, *"we have fasted and God doesn't see"* reveals an approach to fasting as if it were a meritorious act that God will have to reward, or again in verse 3b one which gives an advantage for oneself over others while careless of their rights.

Verse 4 shows a person full of bitterness resulting from the self-denial in which there is no joy in pleasing God. The result of imposing restraints by abstemiousness is to produce an irritable anger and contentiousness, seen in verse 5; this in turn gives rise to sanctimonious posturing and the obsequious hanging of the head and wearing of religious garments that all parade one's fasting and self-righteousness in order to be seen of men – Jesus, centuries later, would say in Matthew 6:16-18 that this is not the fast God has chosen. His chosen fast is meant to raise our prayers to God's heart (v.4b) but fasting unaccompanied by the social righteousness of verses 6 and 7 is no fasting at all, but merely a hypocritical religious cover to one's own selfishness and indifference to the needs of others. This passage does not reject fasting, it emphasises that only when we are loving our fellow human beings and are concerned with their interests will fasting work in lifting our prayers to God.

Fasting is not a panacea for all spiritual ills or a cloak to cover up our sin against our brothers and sisters. 1 Timothy 4:3 clearly indicates there would be legalistic and false teachers who would misuse fasting in the ways which the Old Testament and Jesus are seeking that we should avoid. This verse is a reminder that there are those who practise fasting in occult circles and other religions, and by so doing are seeking to exert negative spiritual power in the same way as we have seen fasting opens the door for positive spiritual power in the Holy Spirit.

1 Timothy 4:3 also warns us that our fasting must be as Jesus' fasting – led by the Spirit and full of the Holy Spirit that we might exert into the world the power, refreshment and goodness of the Spirit of our God. *"The Spirit of the Lord is upon me, because he has anointed me to preach the gospel to the poor, he has sent me to proclaim release to the captives, and recovery of sight to the blind, to set free those who are down-trodden, to proclaim the favourable year of the Lord"* (Luke 4:18-19).

There are four classes or types of fasting if they are defined by the content of each class. However, two other categories will be added in order to cover comprehensively all areas of understanding.

1. Supernatural Fasts

It has already been seen that Moses and Elijah were sustained by God for long periods without food and water. A human being can survive only three days without water, consequently there may be times when God leads into fasts of this kind which could only possibly be sustained by his supernatural energy and power. It would be foolish to seek to accomplish a long fast which excluded water or any liquids if the person was not led by the Holy Spirit into such an activity. There are outstanding cases of imposed fasts on prisoners and martyrs who have been sustained by God for extreme lengths of time.

2. Absolute Fasts

This is where no food or water is taken and would be for a maximum of three days as we have seen. In Esther 4:16 and Acts 9:9 we get this kind of fasting for short periods.

3. Normal Fasts

In normal fasts water or other liquids are taken. These can be for considerable lengths of days, scripturally up to forty days, and some people, of course, have fasted longer than that. Or they may be for a short period, just one day, or even missing merely one meal. Jesus obviously fasted forty days in this kind of way in Matthew 4.

4. Partial Fasts

These are fasts in which there is an abstention from certain types of food as undertaken by Daniel (Daniel 1:8, Daniel 10:2ff). Numbers 6:3, 4 show how the Nazarite fasted from certain foods and drink. John the Baptist seemed to have undertaken a self-imposed fast from luxury foods as he lived in the desert, existing it appears on locusts and wild honey (Matthew 3:4).

With the proviso of course that these are all engaged in under the leading of the Holy Spirit, such fasts are open to Christians. However, we need to consider two further categories.

5. Public and National/Church Fasts

Although the church, like Israel, has instituted and commanded compulsory fast days this does seem to be contradictory to the spirit of Jesus' voluntary fasting. However, if not enforced, a church or national fast would be acceptable as a corporate exercise. An Old Testament example of a national fast day would be the story of Jonah and Nineveh, when the king commanded a fast throughout all his capital city (Jonah 3:6ff). For centuries the Roman Catholic Church commanded fasting from meat on Fridays; this has, however, in more recent years, been changed and is obligatory only throughout Lent. Other churches have maintained Ash Wednesday and Good Friday as days for church fastings throughout their communions. The Greek Orthodox church has four seasons of fasting in its church calendar. A day of fasting was once proclaimed in Britain at the threatened invasion of Napoleon. These are examples of what I have called public or national church fastings.

6. Imposed Fasts

These are not self-imposed, but fasts which circumstances force upon the recipients. It would seem from experiences like Acts 28 in the storm that the sailors had a fast imposed upon them; in other situations in Scripture one could imagine that if the response in these circumstances of obligation was towards God, then there also could be spiritual value in them.

4

Fasting Throughout
Church History

Teachers and leaders throughout church history have encouraged, advocated and practised fasting, generally pointing out that asceticism and self-righteousness should be avoided.

1. Early Church

Polycarp, in his letter to the Philippians, advocated his readers to be "sober unto prayer and constant in fastings".

Irenaeus, in a letter to Pope Victor in 195 AD said, "Some fast one, some two or more days of Holy Week, some forty hours (crucifixion until Easter sunrise); this variety of observance is of long standing and existed in the time of our ancestors."

The Didache, an early manual of Christian teaching, advocated fasting "for the ones who persecute you"; it also encouraged baptismal candidates to fast for one or two days before their baptism and in general encouraged fasting on Wednesdays and Fridays, not Mondays and Thursdays like the hypocrites!

As mentioned earlier in 128AD **Aristides** reported to Emperor Hadrian that Christians fasted two or three days and gave the food they saved to the poor.

Tertullian in his book *On Fasting* in 208 AD extolled fasting as a weapon to fight the worst devils.

Ambrose (340-397 AD), Bishop of Milan, encouraged Christians to follow Jesus' example by fasting in order to be strong against the devil's temptations.

2. Reformation and Beyond

Martin Luther (1483-1546) sought to restore a biblical

perspective to fasting – that it should be voluntary and private. He writes, "Genuine Christian fasting is a fruit of repentance, it helps to keep the flesh in check, and is a fine outward training in preparing to receive God's grace."

Matthew Henry (1662-1714), the author of the famous Bible commentary, regretted that fasting was now neglected among Christians. He gave four reasons why it was important: "It secures God's power to assist us, it sharpens prayer, it demonstrates humiliation before God and it controls the body."

John Wesley (1703-1791): "Some have exhorted religious fasting beyond all Scripture and reason, others have utterly disregarded it". It is known that John Wesley refused to ordain to the Methodist ministry those who did not fast two days each week. He is also reputed to have said that "One who never fasts will no more enter heaven than one who never prays!"

David Brainerd (1718-1747) set aside days to fast and pray for his ministry.

William Bramwell (1759-1818) fasted to conquer his attachment to worldly goods.

Charles Finney (1792-1875) would fast and pray for a day whenever he felt devoid of the power of God.

Charles Spurgeon (1834-1892) wrote "Our seasons of fasting and prayer at the (Metropolitan) Tabernacle have been high days indeed; never has heaven's gate stood wider; never have our hearts been nearer to the central Glory."

3. Twentieth Century

Many Christian biographies record the accounts of the results of fasting in the lives of church leaders and workers. Included here are testimonies from contemporary church life.

a) J is a busy mother of four young children. She was challenged about fasting when she noticed that Jesus said *"When you fast..."* not *"If you fast..."*. So she asked God how to fit it in – and came to the point of believing that the response was whatever she could manage. She decided to fast weekly as a sign of her desire to see more of the power of God, his purposes, and understanding of him released into her life and situation.

Having done this for some time she explains, "Fasting is definitely powerful – though it doesn't twist God's arm. Sometimes when I have had narrow expectations of how he should respond, I have felt disappointed. But when we seek him, he is always faithful, and his answers come.

"I have found there are definite rewards of fasting – which God gives as and when he is ready. It has built faith in my life, God has spoken to me, and I have received promises and reassurance."

Normally she sets aside time for prayer on her fasting days. But with her busy schedule she has found fasting worthwhile even when it is difficult to squeeze in much prayer.

She has also been surprised to find that her occasional longer fasts have been easier to handle physically than her regular fasts. "Sometimes, when you have decided to fast yourself and it's a real struggle, it can be best to let it go. Sometimes I have even forgotten at lunch time on my regular fast day and eaten, but I have not let that condemn me – but committed it to God.

"So you shouldn't get hung up about it. Even fasting one meal – or say, television programmes – is effective if done with faith."

Fasting has brought more discipline to her life, but mainly she has found fasting has focused her priorities. "It's a sign of the importance you place on seeing God's Kingdom and God's will released – that you take this seriously. Fasting acknowledges the true source of life. You are saying to God: I can do without food, but I can't do without your word."

b) A and his three team mates were frustrated by six months of evangelism without results. Their hunger to see God working in greater measure and desperation about the situation drove them to fast for a month. The following five months saw 25 people become Christians and 60 people receive healing of different sorts. "It was a definite breaking-out of the supernatural", A explains.

That was several years ago. Since then he has continued with fasting – in some years fasting once a week, in others doing two or three longer fasts, and sometimes practising what he calls "restraint days", or partial fasts.

His motivation for fasting has remained his hunger to see the glory of God moving powerfully. Through the years there has been an overall lesson, "Fasting should be for the Lord – for his glory to be revealed, and not for things."

Even apart from the release of revelation of Jesus, and of supernatural power in people's lives, A identifies a number of results of fasting. It has brought purity and obedience – both for himself and those he is involved with. "Fasting brings spiritual issues to the surface – perhaps an echo of the way it purges the body of poisons – and God brings change to hearts." He also senses fasting has brought greater inner peace, and the release of spiritual gifts in his life.

He has found that fasting by teams brings unity. "The team dimension also protects from legalism, or getting into fasting and abstinence for its own sake."

Especially for fasts of longer than three days, A advises working in teams, or at least having a trusted friend who knows about the fast and is praying with you through it. "It is not wise to embark on a long fast alone, especially if you have not done much fasting before."

c) B had been praying for a woman on and off for two years. She had had some terrible childhood experiences that had locked her into a private world of fear and hate. But B had come to a blockage; the woman was quite sick and asking for help, but B did not know why she was sick. He says, "So I fasted, for a day or so. During the fast the Lord gave me a sentence which I shared with her. She told me it was something she regularly said about herself. I then told her to write down all the self-curses she had at one time or another spoken over herself. She wrote down over forty! She repented, the dam broke and twenty-four hours later she was healed from the sickness they had brought."

B describes another occasion: "We fasted all day, with worship, to prepare for street evangelism in the town. It was unlike any other time of evangelism I had ever recalled. We felt we were propelled out by the Holy Spirit and found ourselves worshipping in the market place. We had a power and response unlike any other; clapping, laughter, joy, even from all the local folk standing around. It was as though God was so pleased with us for honouring him, that he was giving us all he could, to help us."

d) An active Christian writes: "When I go on a prolonged fast I make it a habit to write out the areas that I am looking for breakthrough in, before I fast and as it proceeds. As the results are often not immediate, this record serves as a reminder to me of what I have asked the Lord about. Afterwards I continue the record, to note what breakthrough I have seen in which areas. The written account always serves as a testimony to God's faithfulness."

e) A Christian counsellor reports: "A woman came to me who had no energy; she was totally unable to cope with the day's demands and said she was close to "cracking up". It was quite obvious, talking to her husband, that the strain on the family was intolerable. All she wanted to do was sleep all day. I sought the Lord for knowledge but he gave me none, except to tell her to fast. She had never done this in her life. But since she had tried everything else, she stopped eating, resigned herself to feeling sick and went to bed. By the end of the first day, she began to feel energy in her body and couldn't stay in bed any longer. By the second day she was feeling quite well and began to tackle the backlog of housework. By the third day, on a diet of water, she was feeling better than she had done for many years. I suggested she go for blood tests to discover to what food she was allergic. She had a very strong allergic reaction to wheat, but instead of it affecting her in a "hyper" way, it would send her to sleep. She stopped eating bread and all of its by-products. She has lived a normal life ever since."

f) A church member involved in church planting writes: "When planting a new congregation in the centre of a London housing estate, we set aside a week of prayer and fasting to see breakthrough prior to beginning evangelism. Some eighteen team members participated, sometimes missing a meal, sometimes fasting for a longer period. We also met for early morning prayer walks around the area during the fast. One of the focal points of the prayer walking was a local pub, which we knew had been a centre for drug-trading in the area and represented a stronghold of the enemy. As a direct result of this time and immediately afterwards, we were given an invitation by the landlady of the pub, to use some of the attached rooms for a Christmas lunch and entertainment for the elderly folk on the estate, who made up a large proportion of the population. One hundred and twenty people attended and the landlady herself provided all the food free of charge! It proved to be a strategic event in the launching of the congregation."

g) This same Christian writes: "I make a habit of fasting to see breakthrough in evangelism. The major benefit I notice is that it sharpens my sensitivity to the release of knowledge through the Holy Spirit. One example of this was during a week of prayer and personal fasting, I was part of a small group doing evangelism in high-rise flats. One lady opened the door to us and said she could not talk with us because she was not well. As she said this I heard a phrase from the Lord – "spiritualist church". I asked if she had ever attended one. Surprised, she said that she had, for the first time three months previously. We then asked her when her illness started – and it was at the same time. When I looked at her, I could literally see a black cloud over her head. We felt there was a curse over her life as a result of attending this church and explained to her the connection. We were able to leave her with some literature and a contact number. This revelation of the cause of the sickness in the woman's life was a direct result of the fast that I was undertaking at the time."

h) A liberal pastor, one who took the Scriptures and their authority lightly, was called in to help a woman said to be demonised. He had a high profile through a television programme in his country, and in his own estimation "thought well of himself". His utter failure to help the woman humbled him. He fasted and found power to deliver the lady. This was followed by six months of regular prayer and fasting with the result of a God-honouring trust in Scripture and subsequent powerful ministry.

These testimonies from ordinary church members and one full-time pastor show the widespread practice of fasting and its varieties of benefits. God is restoring to his Church, his mind and his practices for the recovery of biblical Christianity amongst all the people of God, not just for an isolated mystic or outstanding saint!

One aspect of this recovery has been the emphasis which fasting has received from the twentieth century pentecostal/charismatic movements. Whilst some advocates of fasting like the evangelist/teacher Franklin Hall have been considered as extreme, seemingly suggesting that fasting is the cure of all spiritual ills, nonetheless, fasting as opposed to gluttony is regarded in this movement as the norm of Christian practice and is the milieu in which spiritual gifts may be expected to arise. Franklin Hall considered that the "tapering down of the revival of the 1950's was attributable to the lack of fasting, and to spiritual coasting by the leaders".[9]

In the light of these testimonies and Franklin Hall's remarks we must take seriously the renewed emphasis that the Spirit of God has brought to the Church, highlighting the teaching of Jesus and the commitment to God's purposes that fasting implies. We want to participate in, and contribute to, the current revival movement of God taking place in the world looking forward to the return of our Lord Jesus Christ.

[9]*Dictionary of Pentecostal and Charismatic Movements*, art. Franklin Hall, pp346 (Zondervan, 1988).

Practical Guidelines

1. Begin gradually, maybe in a partial way; not over-eating beforehand to compensate!

2. Withdrawal from coffee/tea can cause headaches – possibly drink water/fruit juices before a fast.

3. Focus on the spiritual, not on the physical; on the benefits and opportunities, not the lost meals.

4. An increase in mouth and body odour may be experienced – peppermints and showers should deal with them!

5. Physical process involved in a longer fast

   Days 1–3:   some discomfort, hunger pains, cleansing of built-up toxic substances in the system.

   Days 4–6:   hunger subsiding; possibly some dizziness and feeling cold.

   Days 7 onwards: should feel stronger; physically, the best part of the fast; feeling spiritually alert.

   Hunger pains generally return between 21 and 40 days, and signal that the body's reserves are used up.

6. A fast of more than a day or so should be broken gradually.

7. Fuller details are given in the books by Arthur Wallis and Richard Foster (see "Further Reading"*).

Further Reading

Chatham, R. D. *Fasting – a Biblical-Historical Study* (Bridge Publishing, 1987).

Cross, F. L. (Ed) *Oxford Dictionary of the Christian Church* (OUP, 1958).

*Foster, Richard *Celebration of Discipline* (Chapter 4) (Hodder, 1978).

Hall, Franklin *The Fasting Prayer* (1954).

Lindsay, Gordon *Prayer and Fasting* (Christ for the Nations, Dallas, 1972).

Maloney, George A. *A Return to Fasting* (Dove Publications, 1974).

Smith, David R. *Fasting: A Neglected Discipline* (New Wine Press, 1988).

*Wallis, Arthur *God's Chosen Fast* (Kingsway, 1968).

Wesley, John *Sermon XXII (on Matthew 6:16-18)* (Epworth Press).

Willard, Dallas *The Spirit of the Disciplines* (Harper & Row, 1988) pp116-168.

If you have enjoyed this book and would like to help us to send a copy of it and many other titles to needy pastors in the **Third World**, please write for further information or send your gift to:

Sovereign World Trust, P.O. Box 777, Tonbridge, Kent TN11 9XT, United Kingdom

or to the **'Sovereign World'** distributor in your country. If sending money from outside the United Kingdom, please send an International Money Order or Foreign Bank Draft in STERLING, drawn on a **UK** bank to **Sovereign World Trust**.